Tess Went to Work

Martin Reed
Illustrated by Virginia Gray

One day, Tess went to work
with her dad.

Library Hours

10:00 – 8:00	Monday to Friday
10:00 – 5:00	Saturday and Sunday

3

Dad helped people find books.

So did Tess.

Reading Corner

Dad helped people use computers.

So did Tess.

Dad helped people
check out books.

So did Tess.

Dad helped people put books away.

So did Tess.

"I had fun at work today," said Tess.

"So did I!" said Dad.